RESOURCE CENTRE
WESTERN ISLES LIBRARIES

Readers are requested to take great care of the [...] possession, and to point out any defects that they may notice in them to the Librarian.
This item should be returned on or before the latest date stamped below, but an extension of the period of loan may be granted when desired.

DATE OF RETURN	DATE OF RETURN	DATE OF RETURN
1 1 JUL 2014		
3 1 MAR 2016		
2 6 MAY 2017		
3 1 OCT 2017		
2 7 JUL 2018		
3 1 MAR 2020		
3 0 SEP 2020		
3 1 MAR 2021		

WITHDRAWN

WITHDRAWN

KU-071-229

WESTERN ISLES
LIBRARIES
30475122⌐
J574.92

34134 00191794 4
Leabharlainn nan Eilean Siar

J574.92

30475122⌐

SCHOOL
LIBRARY
STOCK

L O C A [...] A T S

SEA [...] RE

Nigel Hester

W
FRANKLIN WATTS
LONDON • SYDNEY

This edition 2004

Franklin Watts
96 Leonard Street
London EC2A 4XD

Franklin Watts Australia
45-51 Huntley Street
Alexandria
NSW 2015

Copyright © 1992

First published as Nature Watch: The Living Seashore
Editor: Su Swallow
Designer: K and Co
Illustrations: Angela Owen, Ron Haywood
Picture Research: Sarah Ridley
Phototypeset by Lineage Ltd, Watford

Photography:
Heather Angel 10c, 12l, 18c, 22b, 23; Bruce Coleman Ltd 5tl, 24b,
29 (top inset); Nigel Hester 4bl, 5tr, 5b, 11cl, 12tr, 12tb, 13tl, 16t, 16
(inset), 21bl, 22c, 26tr, 26bl, 27tl; Eric and David Hosking 11tl, 11tr,
14t, 14 (bottom inset), 15; Frank Lane Picture Agency 7, 13tr, 13b,
14 (top inset), 17t, 23 (bottom inset), 24t, 26br, 28t; Natural History
Photographic Agency 15 (inset left), 15 (inset right), 19tl, 27r;
Oxford Scientific Films 4t, 4br, 10b, 11cr, 16b, 18t, 19tr, 19b, 20t,
20c, 20b, 22t, 24b, 28b, 28c, 29t, 29cl; Survival Anglia 14br, 17, 21t,
21br, 23 (centre inset); Barrie Watts 10t; ZEFA 23 (inset top)

All rights reserved. No part of this publication may be reproduced, stored in a retrieval system,
or transmitted in any form or by any means, electronic, mechanical, photocopy, recording or
otherwise, without the prior written permission of the copyright owner.

Front Cover: Natural History Photographic Agency (main picture),
Oxford Scientific Pictures (inset left), Frank Lane Picture Agency (inset right).

A CIP catalogue record for this book is available from the British Library

ISBN: 0 7496 5658 1

Printed in Belgium

CONTENTS

What kind of seashore?   **4**
Between sea and land – 1   **6**
Between sea and land – 2   **8**
Life in a rock pool   **10**
Plants on the cliff   **12**
Birds of the cliff   **14**
Life on a pebble beach   **16**
Life on a sandy beach   **18**
Life on the sand dunes   **20**
Life on the mudflats   **22**
Life in the harbour   **24**
Man and the sea   **26**
Beachcombing   **28**
Field guide   **30**
Index   **32**

WHAT KIND OF SEASHORE?

Do you live close to the sea? Do you ever spend holidays by the sea? What kinds of seashore do you visit? This book tells you about some of the plants and animals that live by the sea, and where to look for them. Some large plants and animals, such as seaweeds and seagulls, are easy to find. Other kinds of wildlife, such as worms and some shellfish, are tiny and hidden from view.

The seashore may be mainly rocks, sand, pebbles or mud. The variety of plants and animals living on the seashore depends on the type of seashore, and whether it is sheltered or exposed to the waves.

Rocky shores *(above)*, cliffs *(below left)* and sandy shores *(below)* are home to different kinds of plants and animals. Rock crevices, pools, seaweed and sand all offer hiding places for small creatures. Cliffs and sand dunes are nesting places for many birds.

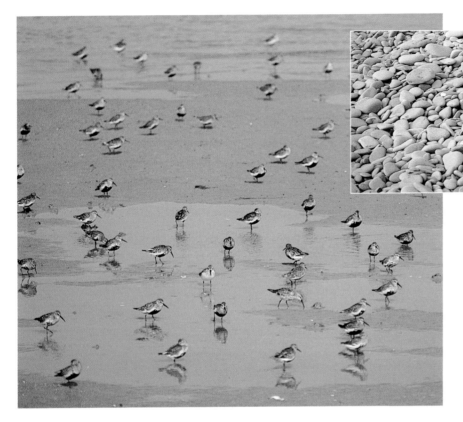

The sound of calling birds is common on muddy shores *(left)*. They feed on the creatures that live in the mud.

Most of the wildlife on pebbly shores *(above)* is found nearest the land, away from the waves that move the pebbles. Harbours *(below)* provide a fairly sheltered spot for seashore life.

Rocky shores with pools are good places to explore, with plenty of wildlife. Pebble shores appear to have very little life, but some plants and animals do manage to live on the pebbles, which are constantly shifting as the tide goes in and out.

Many of the creatures on sandy and muddy shores spend most of the time living underground. You can see where they live from clues that they leave on the surface. Birds visit these seashores to find food. The plants that grow on them have to adapt to salty water, and to dry conditions when the tide goes out.

BETWEEN SEA AND LAND – I

Plants and animals that live on the seashore are adapted to survive all kinds of extreme conditions. When the tide goes out they may be exposed to drying winds, hot sun, heavy rain and, in winter, frost.

The tide uncovers the shore twice a day. Twice a month tides rise higher and fall lower. These are called spring tides. During a spring tide, the sea retreats a long way, exposing much of the shore. This is the best time to explore the shore.

Rocky shores can be divided into four zones: the lower shore, the middle shore, the upper shore and the splash zone. The plants and animals that live on the lower shore are only exposed for a short time by the tide. Those high up on the beach remain uncovered for long periods.

On the lower shore, thick beds of seaweed give protection to many soft-bodied animals and shellfish. On the middle shore, where the water moves more rapidly, most creatures are protected by hard shells and are firmly attached to the rocks.

Seaweeds take in food from the water through their fronds (like leaves). They cling to rocks by a root-like holdfast. Oarweed has a branched holdfast and strap-like fronds. It grows in forests on the lower shore with other seaweeds such as sea belt. They belong to a group of seaweeds known as kelp.

Blue-rayed limpets are shellfish that live in kelp beds. They feed on seaweed and on other animals.

Dulse, a red seaweed, has a disc-like holdfast. It is found on rocks and on kelp stalks.

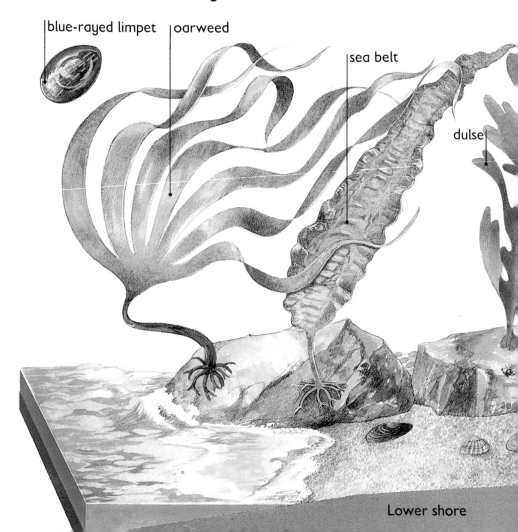

blue-rayed limpet   oarweed   sea belt   dulse

Lower shore

▽ Mussels attach themselves to rocks with tiny threads. People collect mussels to eat.

The pink-purple fronds of laver turn black when they are exposed to the air. In Japan, this seaweed is grown and eaten as a vegetable.

Sea lettuce has pale green fronds that are nearly transparent. It clings to rocks with a disc-like holdfast and is often found close to river mouths.

△ Some seaweeds are collected and cooked as a vegetable, or used in food products.

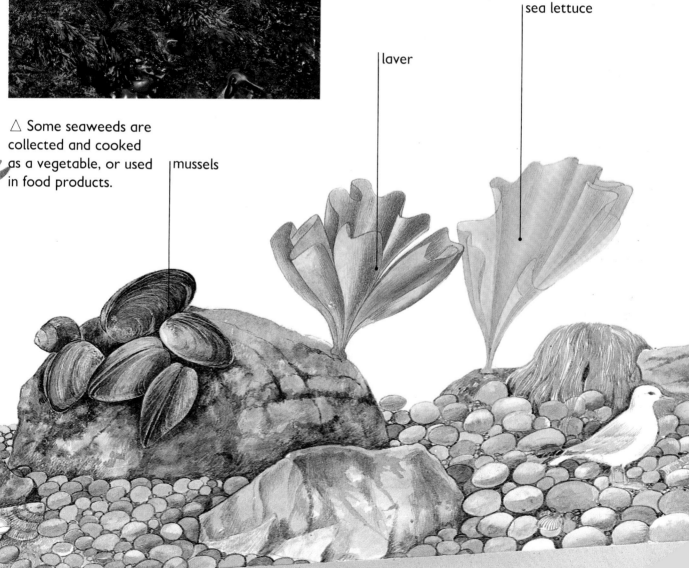

sea lettuce

laver

mussels

Middle shore

During high tide, the rocks of the upper shore are pounded by the waves. At other times, the plants and animals that live there have to survive long periods exposed to the wind and sun. The most abundant plant in this zone is the channelled wrack. It anchors itself in cracks in the rocks to withstand the action of the waves. At low tide, the edges of the fronds curve inwards to retain moisture and prevent the plant from drying out.

Many animals find life too dangerous on the upper shore. Acorn barnacles survive by fixing themselves

When under water, pairs of air bladders help the fronds of bladder wrack to drift up towards the light.

Knotted wrack is common on sheltered seashores, on the middle and upper shores. It can grow to more than 3m long.

Whelks extend a long tube, called a siphon, to find barnacles and mussels on which they feed.

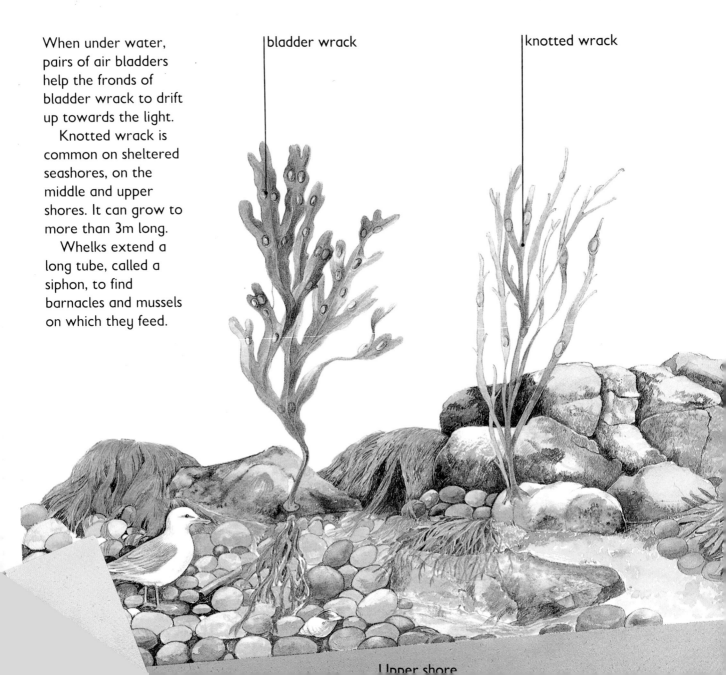

bladder wrack

knotted wrack

Upper shore

permanently to rocks. They feed at high tide; tiny filaments reach out of the top of the shell to catch plankton. When the sea retreats, they close their shells with a chalky plate to keep moisture in.

The highest zone, the splash zone, gets very wet only at high spring tides. It is a harsh place to live. It can be lashed by strong winds and soaked in salt spray. Plants and animals have to hide in cracks in the rocks. Some of the animals only come out to feed at night. During the day they risk being caught by shore crabs and seabirds.

Channelled wrack is named after the way its fronds curve in to form channels.

The small periwinkle is common high up on exposed shores, but it enters the sea to breed.

The sea slater is related to shrimps and crabs. It feeds on dead plant matter.

Black, yellow, green and reddish lichens grow in bands on rocks in the splash zone.

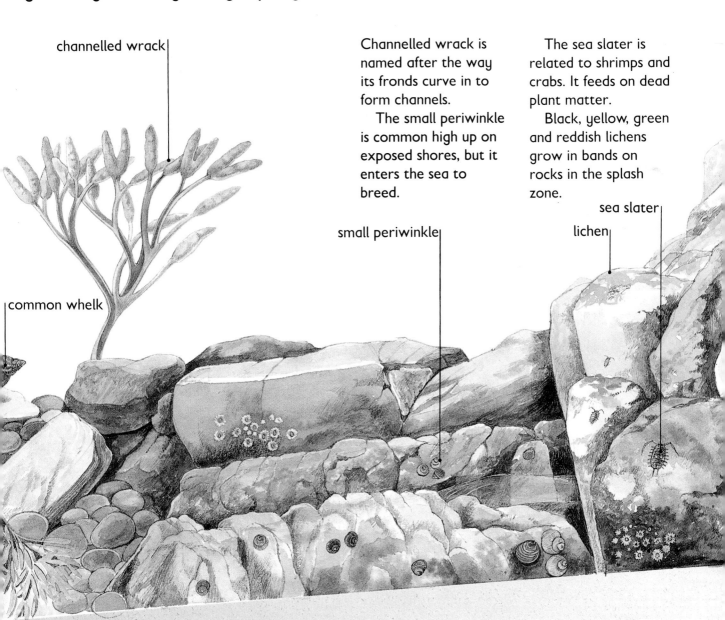

channelled wrack

common whelk

small periwinkle

sea slater

lichen

Splash zone

Hollows form where soft rocks are eroded (worn away) by the action of the waves. These hollows are left full of water when the tide retreats. Life in these pools can be difficult. The sun quickly warms the water, so the plants and animals have to tolerate large variations in water temperature. The salinity (salt content) also varies. As water evaporates in the sun, the water that is left becomes more and more salty.

△ The common starfish, like most starfish, has five arms. It has no head, but its mouth is in the centre of its body. It feeds on mussels, which it pulls apart with its powerful arms.

△ The blenny is common in rock pools. It hides by covering its body in weeds and rock fragments.

▷ The velvet crab is named after the covering of fine hairs on its shell. The hind legs are flattened like paddles for swimming sideways.

Sea anemones (*above* beadlet, *right* snakelocks) feed on small fish and shrimps, which they sting and paralyse with their tentacles. Out of water, the tentacles are drawn in.

The limpet *(top)* clings to rocks with a strong foot which acts like a suction pad. The limpet, and the common periwinkle *(above)* feed on seaweed, using their rough tongue to rasp the plants.

Pools on the lower shore are very similar to the seabed. Large edible crabs, and even lobsters, are sometimes left stranded in these pools. Some fish are safer here than in the open sea.

The best pools are usually found on the middle shore, and may be fringed with a beautiful red seaweed. The bright green seaweed of upper shore pools often hides many insects.

Pool watch

Go to a rocky shore at low tide. Look out for some limpets or dog whelks. If you mark a group of shells with a small spot of paint you can track their movements. Return at the next low tide to see how many have moved away.

Drop a piece of fish or meat into a rock pool. Wait quietly and see what animals emerge from the shadows to eat the titbit.

PLANTS ON THE CLIFF

Not all cliffs support plants. Hard rocks such as granite do not erode very quickly and have few cracks and crevices so not many plants can take root. Cliffs formed of softer rocks have a wider variety of plant life.

All cliff plants have to survive salty sea spray and strong winds. On the cliff top, the soil layer is usually very thin and dries out quickly in summer.

Many birds use cliffs for nesting. The large quantities of droppings, called guano, which they produce can affect the cliff plants. Guano is rich in nitrogen which acts as a fertiliser on plants and makes them grow stronger. But where seabird colonies are very large, the soil becomes loose and plants may disappear from the cliffs.

Thrift or sea pink (*left*, above the nesting kittiwake) grows in tight cushions. It has thin, needle-like leaves to retain moisture. The flowers of sea campion (*above*) can withstand very high levels of salt. Stonecrop (*below*), with its thick, fleshy leaves, grows in dense mats on rocky cliffs.

△ Lichens, which are simple plants, cling tightly to the steep faces of some cliffs. Snails graze this colourful coating. Cliff top flowers attract many insects.

▷ The dark green fritillary feeds on the nectar of violets that grow in the short turf.

The grass on cliff tops and ledges is usually kept very short by rabbits grazing. Some shrubs, such as bramble and gorse, can grow in the shallow soil. Most cliff plants have become specially adapted to prevent them drying out. Some grow in compact cushions, which helps to retain the moisture in the soil around the plant roots. Others have a waxy covering over the stems and leaves to hold in the water.

△ Grassland on cliff tops is often heavily grazed by rabbits. Cliffs are fairly safe places for rabbits.

There are few predators on the coast, and little disturbance from people.

During the spring cliffs become noisy, busy places as seabirds arrive to nest on the cliff top and on the face. They choose remote places to breed, and often nest in huge colonies. Each nesting pair guards the territory around its own nest. Many of these birds spend the rest of the year flying over the open sea.

Some seabirds build nests. Gulls build rather scruffy nests, while kittiwakes build strong, well-shaped nests. Guillemots build no nest at all – they lay their eggs on ledges.

△ The great black-back gull, one of the largest shore birds, is a fast and powerful flyer. It sometimes chases other seabirds and forces them to give up their food.

▷ Cormorants (*top left*) sometimes make their nests at the foot of cliffs. They can often be seen perched on rocks, with their wings outstretched to dry them. Gannets (*top right*) build strong nests because the young stay in the nest for several months. They catch fish by diving into the sea from 30m or more up in the air. Puffins (*main picture*) nest in burrows in cliffs.

◁ The herring gull (*inset, top*) nests on the tops of cliffs. Outside the breeding season it is found anywhere on the coast. It scavenges for food at ports, rubbish dumps and even sewage outfalls.

◁ Kittiwakes (*inset, bottom* and *main picture*) nest on ledges on the cliff face. They collect water plants and plaster them into cracks with mud. They tread on this plant heap to make a hollow in the middle.

Kittiwakes are named after the call they make at breeding time.

LIFE ON A PEBBLE BEACH

The plants on a pebble beach usually have plenty of fresh water. The shingle retains the morning dew and rainwater very well. The biggest problem for these plants is the constant movement of the pebbles, caused by the waves. Young seedlings are easily damaged before they can grow to full size. Nearer the land, the shingle is more stable. Lichens are one of the first colonisers of shingle beaches. As the lichens grow, the spaces between the pebbles fill with grit and pieces of shell. Nutrients arrive from decaying matter washed up by the sea. Gradually, plants are able to take root in this simple soil.

△ Lichens grow in bands parallel to the shore. Each band is a different type of lichen, and depends on the amount of salt in the air.

△ It is said that the people of Aldeburgh on the east coast of England once survived a famine by eating the seeds of the sea pea.

◁ The oyster plant grows close to the ground on shingle beaches. Its oval fleshy leaves taste of oysters and so give the plant its name. Golden samphire *(below)* grows in clumps on shingle.

As more and more plants become established, they help to stabilise the shingle. Most shingle plants have long woody roots that can withstand the movement of the pebbles. These roots go deep into the shingle to anchor the plant and seek out fresh water.

The number of animals that can live on shingle is small. A few insects live close to the plants. Hunting spiders search among the pebbles for prey. Birds are sometimes seen on shingle shores searching for food beneath the pebbles.

The turnstone *(above)* is named after the way it turns over stones looking for small creatures to eat. The ringed plover *(right)* feeds on sandy shores, but it breeds on shingle.

Collecting pebbles
Make a collection of some pebbles with strong markings. Wash and dry them, and paint them with a clear varnish to make their colour vivid.

At first glance, sandy beaches appear to have very little life. But most creatures burrow into the sand when the tide goes out, partly to stay moist and partly to hide from predators. Their hiding places can be detected by trails, casts and hollows in the sand. Finding these clues is quite easy. Finding the animals is much harder. Many sand dwellers can burrow faster than you can dig.

Molluscs are soft-bodied animals protected by one or two shells. Some molluscs, such as cockles and razor shells, burrow in the sand. Large numbers of birds feed on these molluscs and on worms, digging into the sand with their long beaks.

△ Hermit crabs live in old shells on all kinds of shore.

▷ This razor shell is starting to burrow. Look for keyhole-shaped hollows in wet sand to find where they are buried.

◁ The lugworm lives in a U-shaped tube. It sucks in sand at one end, leaving a small hollow on the surface. It takes food from this sand and then squirts the sand out of the other end, leaving a squiggly cast. Sand eels swim near the water's edge, and also burrow into sand. Ragworms burrow too – they have up to 20 teeth for biting their prey. The sea potato, a kind of sea urchin, leaves a dent on the surface where it has burrowed.

ragworm

sand eel

lugworm

cockle

sea potato

The sanderling *(above)* lives on sandy shores, where it runs quickly along the edge of the water looking for food. The little tern *(left)* can hover when searching for small fish. It nests on sandy and pebbly beaches.

▽ Seals are rare visitors to sandy beaches. Pups are born on remote sandbanks or rocky shores.

On broad, flat beaches the wind continually blows the grains of sand towards the land. If any plants can gain a foothold on the sand, then sand dunes begin to form around their roots. Some grasses that can withstand the wind and salt spray spread by sending out underground runners, called rhizomes. The net of rhizomes helps to stabilise the sand. Other plants then take root.

These pioneer plants cause the sand to build up in a low ridge. Marram grass then becomes established, spreading step-by-step up the growing sand dune. The remains of old marram and other debris collect behind the dune. This forms a simple soil for sand sedge, sea holly and other tough plants.

◁ The trailing roots of sea bindweed help to trap the shifting sand. Rabbits like to feed on its flowers.

△ ▷ Sea holly is a member of the carrot family. Its fruits are covered in small hooks.

◁ Sand dunes can become very hot on sunny days. At night, moisture from the sea forms dew. This is a valuable source of water for plants and animals.

Marram grass is one of the most important sand dune grasses. It grows quickly through the sand, which builds up round its stems.

As the dunes grow, sheltered damp areas form between them. Orchids and other marshy plants grow here. Insects such as flies, moths and butterflies visit the dunes to feed on the plants, and hunting spiders and ground beetles hunt their prey among the plant stems. Broken shells provide an important source of calcium for snails, which need it to grow their own shells.

△ The bright flowers of the yellow-horned poppy last for only about two days. The seed pod is the longest of any British plant.

▷ The clouded yellow butterfly flies north from southern Europe in spring to breed. It is found on sand dune flowers.

▽ The six-spot burnet moth is another insect that feeds on the nectar of dune flowers.

Where rivers flow into the sea they deposit large amounts of silt (fine mud). Flat expanses of mud form, called mudflats. Animals and plants that live on them have to tolerate big changes in the salt content of the water. When the tide is out, there is plenty of fresh water from the river. When the tide rises the salt content quickly rises as the sea water mixes with the river water.

In sheltered conditions the mudflats become quite stable. Plants grow on the mud and form a saltmarsh. As debris is trapped around their roots and stems, the level of the saltmarsh rises. As it rises, less seawater covers the marsh at high tide. So more plants become established. Eventually the saltmarsh rises so much that it is covered by seawater only at the highest spring tide.

There is not a wide variety of animals living on the mudflats, but those creatures that do live there occur in huge numbers. One square metre of mud, for example, may contain as many as 60,000 spire shells. The mud is also home to worms and to shore crabs. Fish that feed over mudflats tend to be flat. They glide over the mud at high tide looking for worms to eat.

△ The sea aster is common on saltmarshes. There are two varieties in Britain. The blue-purple variety grows mainly on the western coast. The yellow one grows on the eastern coast.

▷ Empty shells often collect on the edges of the mudflats, sometimes forming a beach of shells.

▽ On mudflats, shore crabs hide under stones or seaweed.

▷ The curlew (top right) has a long, down-turned bill which is ideal for probing deep into the mud. The dunlin (middle right) keeps changing its plumage during the year. It probes the mud rapidly for food. The knot (bottom right and far right) gathers in huge flocks over mudflats from autumn until spring. The flocks appear white and then black as the birds turn and wheel in the sky.

Man-made features such as harbours, piers and breakwaters attract plants and animals that are also found on rocky shores. They spend most of their lives attached to the firm surfaces of timber and stone.

The water around harbours is a good spot to watch for fish. If the seabed is sandy, then flatfish may enter the harbour searching for worms. Other fish will scavenge for debris dropped from fishing boats and gulls may appear, looking for an easy meal. Jellyfish can sometimes be seen sheltering under piers at high tide.

△ The common jellyfish drifts along looking for small fish. It is sometimes washed ashore.

The common gull *(below)* and other gulls are often seen in harbours *(left)*, where they feed on fish remains thrown from fishing boats.

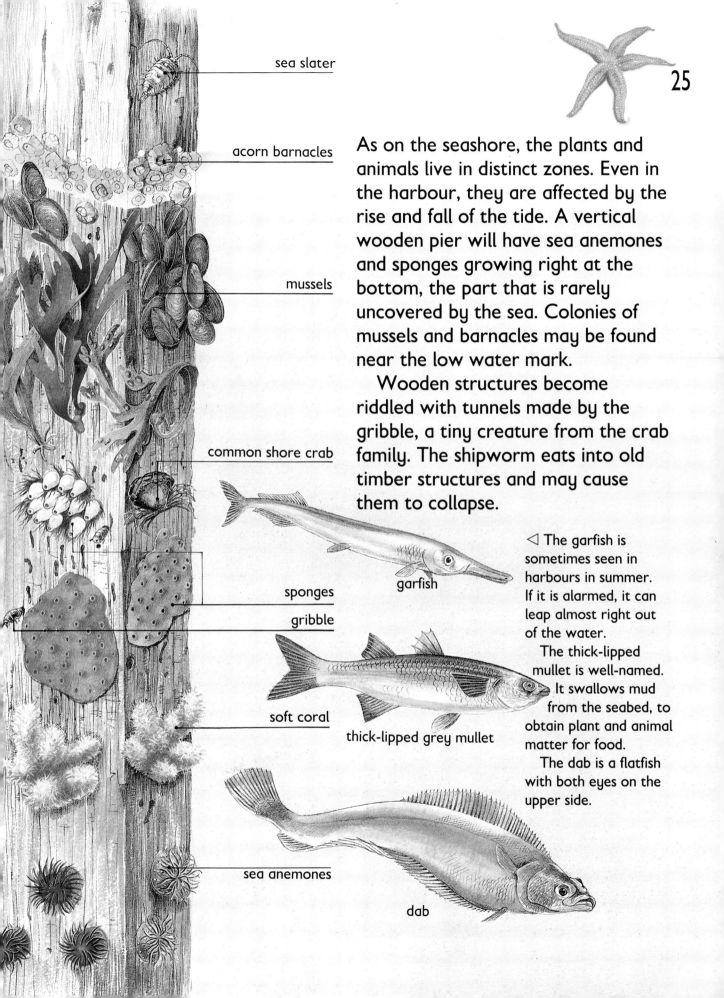

sea slater

acorn barnacles

mussels

common shore crab

sponges

gribble

soft coral

sea anemones

garfish

thick-lipped grey mullet

dab

As on the seashore, the plants and animals live in distinct zones. Even in the harbour, they are affected by the rise and fall of the tide. A vertical wooden pier will have sea anemones and sponges growing right at the bottom, the part that is rarely uncovered by the sea. Colonies of mussels and barnacles may be found near the low water mark.

Wooden structures become riddled with tunnels made by the gribble, a tiny creature from the crab family. The shipworm eats into old timber structures and may cause them to collapse.

◁ The garfish is sometimes seen in harbours in summer. If it is alarmed, it can leap almost right out of the water.

The thick-lipped mullet is well-named. It swallows mud from the seabed, to obtain plant and animal matter for food.

The dab is a flatfish with both eyes on the upper side.

Fishing is an important industry in many countries. Different kinds of fishing boats and a variety of nets are used to catch different kinds of fish. Trawlers pull a large bag-shaped trawl net behind them to catch fish. The net is winched aboard and the fish are packed in ice to keep them fresh until they are sold.

People in Britain eat nearly a million tonnes of fish each year. To produce enough fish for the market, some kinds of fish, such as salmon, trout and some shellfish, are reared on fish farms.

Fishing is also a popular sport. It is important that anglers return small fish to the sea so that they can grow to full size. It is also important not to throw old fishing tackle into the sea. Seabirds can become entwined in old fishing line. But one of the biggest problems for seashore wildlife is oil pollution. Oil spills from ships at sea kill many fish and seabirds each year, and oil slicks that wash ashore destroy all the plants and animals that live there.

Most of the fish we eat *(above)* comes from the sea. Boats *(left)* leave harbours every day in all weathers to catch the fish. Fish farming *(right)* is a new industry which helps to produce enough fish for everyone.

△ Rubbish thrown overboard from ships at sea causes serious pollution to beaches. Plastic containers, drums of dangerous chemicals, ropes and nets all get washed up eventually on the seashore.

▷ Many animals and plants are affected by oil spillages, but seabirds are most at risk. If their feathers become covered in oil they cannot fly, and so they are unable to feed.

Sea facts

 About 97 per cent of the earth's water lies in the oceans and seas.

 The world's longest mountain range stretches under the sea for 16,000km, from Iceland to the Antarctic.

 In the deeper parts of the sea, animals such as shrimps, sponges and squid produce their own lights.

 Starfish can regrow from just one limb, provided a small bit of the body is attached.

 In 1938 fishermen in the Indian Ocean caught a strange-looking fish called a coelacanth. Until then, scientists thought that it had been extinct for millions of years.

 The sting of a sea wasp, a type of jellyfish, can kill a person in a few minutes.

 The hermit crab will often share its home, a discarded whelk shell, with a ragworm.

Many plants and animals, and man-made objects, float about at sea. When the tide comes in some of them are brought on to the seashore. They are left in a line at the high point of the tide. This line of debris is called the strandline or tideline. The strandline is a good place to explore, especially after a storm.

Seaweeds form a large part of the strandline. Although the seaweed will dry out on the surface, underneath it stays quite wet and provides a temporary shelter for small animals. You may find tiny sandhoppers jumping about under the seaweed — they feed on rotting plant material. You may also find the egg cases of fish on the beach.

△ Seaweed collects along the strandline and marks the point reached by the high tide.

△ Spongy balls of common whelk egg cases are often on the strandline. Each round capsule contained an egg.

◁ The egg case of the dogfish is called a mermaid's purse. The tendrils are for attaching the case to seaweed. Most cases washed ashore are empty; the young fish hatch at sea.

The empty shells of crabs and shellfish are common among the remains on the strandline. The bones from cuttlefish are easy to find, too. Old timber from ships may be washed ashore, riddled with holes from shipworm and gribbles. You may be lucky enough to find seeds and fruits washed up from tropical regions. They may have been floating for thousands of kilometres before they reach your seashore.

◁ The sea mouse is a kind of worm, which may be up to 20cm long, with a hairy body. It is sometimes washed ashore.

△ The cuttlefish is related to the octopus. It has good eyesight and grabs its prey with two of its 10 tentacles. It has an internal shell, called a cuttlebone (inset), that is often washed up on the shore.

Seashore treasure

Try making a collection of seashells. Wash them in fresh water and dry them. See how many you can identify.

Birds drop their feathers when they moult. You could collect seabird feathers from the seashore.

Collect different types of seaweed. Wash the plants in fresh water, lay them between sheets of newspaper and weigh them down with heavy, flat pieces of wood. Change the paper every few days. Eventually the seaweed will be perfectly dry and it can then be mounted on card. Try to label each type.

FIELD GUIDE

The kind of seashore life you spot will vary from one kind of beach to another, although some species live on any beach, whether it is rocky, sandy, muddy or even shingle.

Remember that the best time to explore the seashore is at low tide. Find out the times of the tides from the local newspaper. Take a fishing net for exploring rock pools, and return the plants and animals carefully when you have finished looking at them. If you move seaweed or rocks and stones to find animals underneath, put them carefully back in position afterwards.

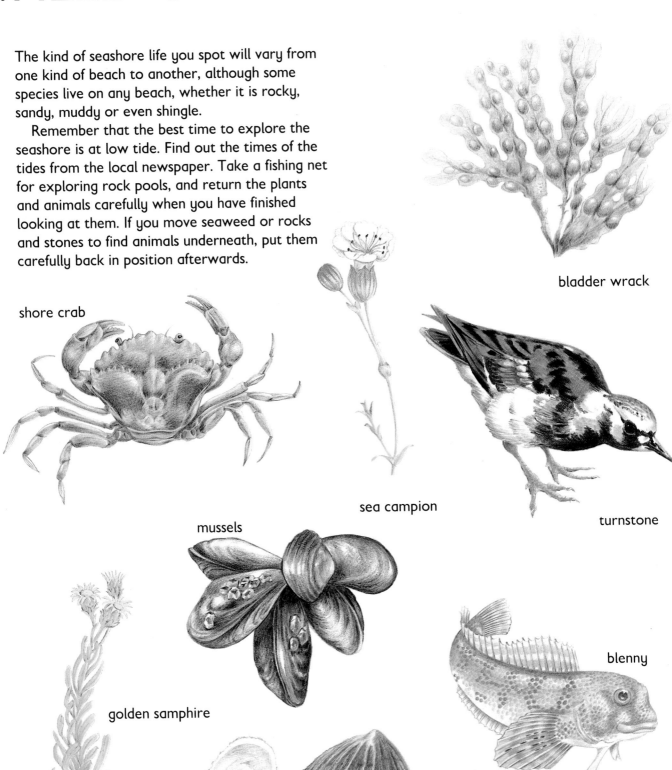

bladder wrack

shore crab

sea campion

turnstone

mussels

blenny

golden samphire

limpet

thrift

cormorant

sea aster

beadlet sea anemone

common starfish

sea belt

hermit crab

herring gull

Spot the plants and insects

Now that you have read about the seashore, test your knowledge and see if you can identify the plants and animals that have appeared at the top of some of the pages in this book. You will find the answers to the quiz on the next page.

Barnacles, acorn 8, 25
Beachcombing 28
Blenny 10, 30
Butterflies 21
    clouded yellow butterfly 21
    dark green fritillary butterfly 13

Cliffs 4, 12, 13, 14
Cockles 18
Coelacanth 27
Cormorant 14, 15, 31
Crabs 9, 29
    hermit crab 18, 27, 31
    shore crab 22, 25, 30
    velvet crab 10
Curlew 22, 23
Cuttlefish 29

Dab 25
Dogfish 28
Dulse 6
Dunlin 22, 23
Dunes, sand 40, 20, 21

Fish farms 26
Fishing 26
Flatfish 24

Gannet 14, 15
Garfish 25
Golden samphire 16, 30
Gribble 29
Guano 12
Guillemots 14
Gulls 14, 24
    common gull 24
    great black-back gull 14
    herring gull 14, 31

Harbours 5, 24, 25

Insects 11, 13, 17

Jellyfish 24, 27

Kelp 6
Kittiwake 12, 14
Knot 22, 23

Laver 7
Lichens 9, 13, 16
Limpets 11, 30
    blue-rayed limpet 6
Lugworm 18

Marram grass 20
Molluscs 18
Moths 21
    six-spot burnet moth 21
Muddy shores 5
Mudflats 22, 23
Mullet, thick-lipped grey 25
Mussels 7, 25, 30

Oarweed 6
Orchids 21
Oyster plant 16

Pebble shores 5, 16, 17
Periwinkle, common 1
    small periwinkle 9
Plankton 9
Plover, ringed 17
Poppy, yellow-horned 21
Puffin 14, 15

Rabbits 13, 20
Ragworm 18, 27
Razor shell 18
Rock pools 4, 5, 10, 11
Rocky shores 4, 5, 6

Saltmarsh 2
Samphire, golden 30
Sand eel 18
Sanderling 19
Sandy shores 4, 17, 18, 19
Sandhoppers 28
Sea anemones 11, 25
    beadlet sea anemone 11
    snakelocks sea anemone 11
Sea aster 22, 31
Sea belt 6, 31
Sea bindweed 20
Sea campion 12, 30
Seagulls 4

Sea holly 20
Sea lettuce 7
Seals 19
Sea mouse 29
Sea pea 16
Sea pink 11
Sea potato 18
Sea slater 9, 25
Sea urchin 18
Seaweeds 4, 6, 7, 11, 22, 28, 29
Shellfish 4, 6, 26, 29
Shrimps 9, 11, 27
Shingle beaches 16, 17
Shipworm 25, 29
Snails 13, 21
Sponges 25, 27
Squid 27
Starfish 27
    common starfish 10, 31
Stonecrop 12
Strandline 28

Tern, little 19
Thrift 12, 31
Tides 6, 8, 9, 10, 22
Trawlers 26
Turnstone 17, 30

Whelks, dog 11
    common whelk 28
Worms 4, 18, 22
Wrack, bladder 8, 30
    channelled wrack 8, 9
    knotted wrack 8

Zones 6, 8, 25

Answers to quiz: page 1 shore crab, p2 golden samphire, p3 cormorant, p5 turnstone, p7 blenny, p9 hermit crab, p11 thrift, p13 mussels, p14 sea belt, p17 bladder wrack, p19 beadlet sea anemone, p21 limpet, p22 sea campion, p25 common starfish, p27 herring gull, p29 sea aster.

PRINTED IN BELGIUM BY proost INTERNATIONAL BOOK PRODUCTION